AF225196

Relational Psychoanalysis

Improve your Social Skills, Overcome Anxiety in Relationships, Boost your Self Esteem and Confidence. From Relationship Trauma to Resilience and Balance

Annie Faison

© Copyright All rights reserved.

This eBook is provided with the sole purpose of providing relevant information on a specific topic for which every reasonable effort has been made to ensure that it is both accurate and reasonable. Nevertheless, by purchasing this eBook, you consent to the fact that the author, as well as the publisher, are in no way experts on the topics contained herein, regardless of any claims as such that may be made within. As such, any suggestions or recommendations that are made within are done so purely for entertainment value. It is recommended that you always consult a professional prior to undertaking any of the advice or techniques discussed within.

This is a legally binding declaration that is considered both valid and fair by both the Committee of Publishers Association and the American Bar Association and should be considered as legally binding within the United States.

The reproduction, transmission, and duplication of any of the content found herein, including any specific or extended information, will be done as an illegal act regardless of the end form the information ultimately takes. This includes copied versions of the work, both physical, digital, and audio unless express consent of the Publisher is provided beforehand. Any additional rights reserved.

Furthermore, the information that can be found within the pages described forthwith shall be considered both accurate and truthful when it comes to the recounting of facts. As such, any use, correct or incorrect, of the provided information will render the Publisher free of responsibility as to the actions taken outside of their direct purview. Regardless, there are zero scenarios where the original author or the Publisher can be deemed liable in any fashion for any damages or hardships that may result from any of the information discussed herein.

Additionally, the information in the following pages is intended only for informational purposes and should thus be thought of as universal. As befitting its nature, it is presented without assurance regarding its prolonged validity or interim quality. Trademarks that are mentioned are done without written consent and can in no way be considered an endorsement from the trademark holder.

Introduction

Most of us reflect on how much we learn, but the willingness to communicate and be present in the middle of assignments is what distinguishes leaders.

Imagine that you're having coffee with a prospective client and that all the while you're chatting, you're responding to text and email at the same while. You speak to the client with your voice, but your eyes are on your phone. You may think that your solutions to the problems of your client are highly valuable, but the next day, the client informs you that they have chosen to go in a different direction, the explanation for that? You're deficient in emotional intelligence.

Relationship intelligence is a potential strategic edge for leaders. "Relational intelligence is the capacity to communicate and be present in the middle of activities," While most of us center our interactions on the information we wish to share, our observable core competencies, IQ is no longer a strategic advantage.

Actually, they are personalities who have the potential to communicate with other people and stand out in the crowd. Relative intelligence, he claims, is about power. "It enhances your power, your appearance, the urge for people to be around you," Relative intellibence can be accomplished by adopting the five-step process. There are five modes that we are passing through during our working day: fifth gear: concentration mode, fourth gear: mission mode, third gear: social mode, second gear: attach mode, first gear: refresh. Shifting through these gears at the right moment is what makes it possible for one to have a cognitive intellect.

UNDERSTAND HOW YOU GET STUCK

You remember the coworker who still turns up at the after-work drinks while always thinking about his to - do list? This man is trapped in the fourth gear: the mission mode and he's having trouble changing to the third gear: the social mode. Understanding what kind of gear you appear to get caught in is the first step in developing your relationship intelligence.

PULL THE TRIGGER

Trigger points during your day, such as the time of day when you interrupt what you're doing and mentally change to a new level, are crucial for increasing your relationship intelligence. It's known that if you didn't have a social intellect, he might come home and stay in his driveway for half an hour chatting on the phone or reading a voice mail job. As he stepped through the door to his home, he was already in the fourth gear: the mission mode instead of the second gear: the communicating mode, as he spends time with his family.

While he was seated at the dinner table, emotionally, he was already running over the list of things he had to do for the day and preparing a list of the activities he needed to do for the next day. "Relational intellibence is about communication," "You're communicating with others by getting in the right gear." It's found that a bridge 2.5 miles from his home is his latest focal point. "As soon as I get to the bridge, I stop talking on the phone, get out of work in my head as much as I can, and start changing to the second gear. I'm beginning to wonder, what do my children need? What does my wife need to do? And when I pull into the driveway, I'm in the right gear at the right time, "he says. Finding a catalyst–a physical marker or a moment–when you're asking yourself to shift directions is the secret to being more relationally knowledgeable.

Deliberately do the job

How many times have you been disturbed by reading this article? Have you stopped to review the email message that shows up on your screen? Did a friend come into your office to ask a question? Relational intellibence will also also increase your productivity by allowing you to be more deeply linked to what you're focused on. A individual with high relational intelligence may respond to an interruption by saying, "I'd love to talk about this, but at the moment, my mind is focused on something else, so I'm not going to be totally with you right now. Will we talk at 2:00 p.m. When would I be completely focused on you?" Being conscious, trying to be there, that's emotional intelligence.

Chapter one

Origins of Relational Intelligence

Relational Intelligence is our capacity as human beings to communicate with others and create trust.

You may have heard about Emotional Intelligence before, and wondered how it contributes to Cognitive Intelligence. Strong emotional intelligence, as we see it, allows relative intellibence to grow and extend. When you're able to recognize and appreciate your feelings and those of others, you're best prepared to develop relationships.

In the modern world of employment, where relational capabilities take priority over technological expertise, Relational Intelligence is the top strategic edge for market success. Previously called a "soft talent" (what HR expert Josh Bersin terms "strength skills") in the workplace, our ability to connect and affect others, create trust, resolve tension, and communicate effectively is more critical than ever. Let's dive a little further into that.

Relational Intellibence is the capacity to develop solid relationships and confidence, given our discrepancies, where good will prevails, in order to accomplish objectives. They represent successful and polite contact and psychological stability that allows us to present ourselves as we are and to make mistakes without fear of reprisal.

Such partnerships begin by recognizing that we are not all equal, that we understand our differences, that we avoid treating them as a challenge, and we turn them into strategic advantages.

In other words, collective intellect is the secret to balancing diversity and promoting a climate of inclusion. And the largest diversity that exists, beyond class, race, religious views and other variations, is our patterns and personality characteristics, our typologies.

At the level of work in particular, Relational Intelligence offers the following benefits: • produces self-knowledge and a strong awareness of the existing abilities and possible fields to be improved to maintain consistency and enhance results.

• Makes it easier for others to understand their differences and optimizes communication • Improve working relationships and develop leadership • Integrate high-self-teams • Strengthens relationships with clients and collaborators in general to promote the achievement of objectives.

Maximize commitment, teamwork and cooperation• Enhance environment, society and outcomes.

What is relational intelligence

A mixture of emotional and ethical intelligence, which includes the capacity to be conscious of and consider our own and others' desires, beliefs, expectations and needs, to differentiate between them, to objectively comment on them, and to use this knowledge to direct one's acts and behavior with respect to others. We have more time, more concentration, less drama, more fun in our lives, and this complex combination means that we can't help but be successful!

Relational Intelligence encompasses abilities such as self-awareness, empathy, knowing multiple viewpoints, physiological and verbal precision, capacity to communicate with others, and controlling feelings. Some of us are better than some in some of these regions.

The good news is that you will think about analytical intelligence. It's more difficult to boost your IQ than your friendship intellect. Relational and emotional competencies require, in particular, pathways that extend from emotional centres to prefrontal lobes. Efficient preparation for relational intelligence relays these loops. Circuit rewiring happens mainly through the self-awareness of social blind spots, the development of new habits, and the use of a feedback mechanism to help the learning.

Relational Intelligence Benefits

Relational Intelligence helps you to improve your social interaction, whether private or personal, which is why the nature of our interaction determines our everyday lives and our desire to excel in our actions.

It is important that we learn how to overcome interpersonal disputes and that we develop empathic skills that help us to strengthen relationships with others. When are we going to do this?

Easy, It is recommended that you examine these 6 skills:

-Control your appearance and your image-Begin by understanding yourself, both in your feelings, emotions and movements, in such a way that you recognize the subtle signals that you give to your interlocutor.

-Improve your capacity for positive influence-Assess your ability and how you can distinguish and leverage it by being creative and unique.

-Improve control of yourself-It is necessary to understand strategies that allow you to help manage or prevent professional circumstances that create or cause anxiety in such a way as to remove counterproductive behaviors.

Harmonious ties with others, beginning with the establishment of an attitude without discrimination and a relationship of trust and respect. Analyze the relationship you share with your colleagues, your bosses and your customers, and learn to listen, consider and look at them in an analytical manner.

Mindful when the relationship with others fails or deteriorates- To learn how to avoid disputes, you have to deal with them at the start, and it is important to recognize commitment or exclusion habits.

Self-knowledge and self-assessment techniques that help you to manage thoughts and emotions, the secret to difficulties

How to develop Relational Intelligence

We need to concentrate on two things in order to improve our Relational Intelligence, First, self-knowledge that helps us to affirm our innate talents and utilize them more frequently, as well as to recognise our blind spots, they appear to work while we're under strain, they're like our "normal." When we do not make them mindful that they may explode adversely and cause responses capable of undermining our relationships.

Firstly, we must accept that we are not all the same, that there are different ways of understanding and experiencing the universe and, above all, that none is better or worse. Our preferred behavioral patterns decide our typology and our knowledge of the root and appreciation for these distinctions in order to take advantage of them constructively is the simplest, quickest and most straightforward way to create positive connections and lasting relationships.

Those with a high degree of Relational Intelligence are people's experts, and the hallmark of those who have it is to anticipate people's reactions in advance. And they are better communicators and better motivators, and they will have more impact over others.

Undoubtedly, Relational Intelligence forecasts success both individually and at work. The nice news is that everyone, totally everybody, will grow our Relational Intelligence and increasing our IQ!

Why is Relational Intelligence relevant in our workplaces

Workplaces are shifting at a dizzying rate and it's hard for companies and individuals to keep up. As Gallup continues to show in their study, the question is not that these developments are coming — it's how to cope with them.

Numerous surveys suggest that while we're more linked than ever in the digital world, we're failing to make the same connection in the physical world. Much as relationships enrich our personal lives, it is also the strength of our work relationships that defines the nature of our jobs and our performance. Stronger partnerships lead to more constructive conversations, more creative approaches and, inevitably, improved market results.

SIGNS OF STRONG RELATIONS

People are open to each other and share their truthful feelings People actively exchange knowledge and collaborate with each other People and teams play with new ideas and venture beyond the box IMPACT ON THE BUSINESS Anxiety of having uncomfortable or delicate discussions is eliminated and cohesion rises Silos are dissolved and people work together.

But what's with the work?

Let's step back and call the elephant in the room here: isn't there a risk that if we rely too hard on relationships, research really isn't going to get done?

Managers have huge tasks to meet, and between the needs of your staff and the needs of your manager, you may be thinking when you're going to have time to give priority to developing Relational intelligence. The positive news is that the relationship-building will not have to come at the expense of decreased team efficiency. On the opposite... Task-oriented leadership is often opposed to relationship-oriented leadership, but we fully agree that they should not have to operate in opposition. In the long run, reflecting on partnerships and maintaining them will lead to higher results and improved outcomes. Like they say, individually you're going further, you're moving back together.

Being relationship-focused does not involve attempting to make sure that everyone is friends, or that there is no conflict or dispute. Indeed, properly handled, building relationships should not prevent confrontation itself, but instead promote protection to discuss concepts and work through confrontation, so that disputes can be overcome and lead to improved outcomes.

Getting individuals with high Emotional Experience on the teams not only leads to a culture of commitment, but also to the development of new and more creative solutions, strengthened team cohesion and cooperation, and a greater sense of common meaning and purpose. That's why it's important that managers promote and cultivate these friendship ties inside and outside their teams.

How do you build Relational Intelligence

How can you create Relational Intelligence on your own or on your own team? There is no hidden formula, but the best way to begin with is sincere curiosity and careful listening.

At our Relational Intelligence workshop at C2 Montreal 2019, in just 90 minutes, we were able to make a clear bond with people who didn't know much about each other before the meeting. The students learned how the practice of their imagination and deep listening motivated them to successfully accomplish the same activity at the conclusion of the session as they did at the outset.

Activities to cultivate empathy and deep listening in a group Practice these activities with the team and help create the true links.

To be heard, not seen Invite people to form groups of 3 or 4 individuals. Tell them to close their eyes and allow them 5 minutes to speak to each other to try and identify 3 aspects they have in common that make their group special or different relative to other groups. It may be awkward at first, but the absence of eye interaction forces people to truly concentrate on what others are doing.

Starting a dialogue Let us sit down in a group and take up any questions they can ask each other. You should continue with low-intensity questions such as: • Should you tell us about one person who has inspired you in your life?

- Would you think the planet is going to be a better or bad place 100 years from now?
- What's new to what you've come to do over the last year?
- Would you share a special memory with us?

There are hundreds of questions like this that people might ask each other for. You should also allow others to respond on their own concerns. It's in the little observations that people make about each other that the bonds begin to develop.

Getting true, and really listening Encourage people to exercise deep listening in pairs. Ask one person(' the sharer') to share a problem that is real for them right now about which they have no resolution. Invite the sharer to talk as their friend(' the listener') listens.

After 3 minutes, advise the audience to respond accordingly, either by staying quiet or by posing important questions. Insist on the fact that the listener will avoid the temptation to come out with suggestions or attempt and console the other person.

Here are few examples of important questions that can be suggested:• What do you feel about the situation?

• Why is it impacting you?

• What really matters to you?

• What's the biggest need for you?

• What are you afraid of?

• What do you know about yourself through this experience?

• What will help you build a sense of optimism for the future?

• When you envision the perfect case, what's going to happen?

Make the pairs swap positions, and encourage everybody to provide an account of the nature of the communication and the impact it had on the sharer.

Chapter Two

Defining your Relationships

Each relationship is special, so people come together for a number of reasons. Part of what determines a good partnership is having a shared vision of both what you want the partnership to be and where you want it to go. And that's something you're just going to learn by talking sincerely and frankly to your friend. Nevertheless, there are also some of the attributes that most stable marriages have in common. Knowing these fundamental values will help keep your partnership positive, satisfying and enjoyable, whatever the goal or the struggle you face together.

You share a positive interpersonal bond with each other. You make each other feel cherished and emotionally happy. There is a distinction between being loved and feeling cherished. If you feel cherished, it makes you feel welcomed and respected by your mate, as anyone truly does. Some couples are trapped in happy coexistence, but the spouses do not even respond to each other emotionally. Although the relationship may appear secure on the surface, a lack of continuing engagement and personal interaction just adds to the gap between two individuals.

You are not scared of (respectful) conflict. Some people work it out gently, while others can lift their voices and argue passionately. But the trick to a good friendship is not to be scared of confrontation. You need to feel free to say issues that concern you without fear of reprisal, and to be able to overcome disagreement without embarrassment, disrespect, or claiming that you are right.

You keep your connections and desires alive outside. Notwithstanding the promises of romantic fiction or film, no one can satisfy all of your needs. In reality, expecting so much from your partner will place an undeserved burden on your relationship. In order to sustain and enrich your romantic relationship, it is important to preserve your own identity outside of your relationship, to preserve relationships with family and friends, and to retain your hobbies and interests.

You should interact freely and frankly. Effective contact is a vital part of every kind of partnership. If both partners know what they want from the relationship and are confident sharing their wants, concerns and wishes, they will build up trust and reinforce the bond between you.

Defining a good relationship

There are many qualities that make up a good, stable working relationship:

• Honesty–this is the basis of a good partnership. When you trust your team and friends, you build a strong partnership that makes you collaborate and connect more effectively. If you trust the people you work with, you will be transparent and truthful about your opinions and acts, and you don't have to waste time and energy by "watching your back."

• Shared Respect — When you love the people you work with, you appreciate their feedback and suggestions, and they appreciate yours. Working together, you will create approaches that are focused on your common experience, knowledge and imagination.

• Mindfulness–this involves taking responsibility for your thoughts and acts. Those that are conscious are vigilant and look out for what they do, so they don't let their own negative feelings influence the people around them.

• Embrace Diversity–People with strong partnerships not only accept diverse personalities and views, they also encourage them. For example, when your peers and colleagues give differing viewpoints than yours, you take the time to hear what they have to say and take into account their input into your decision-making.

• Flexible Contact—We chat every day, whether we send emails and IMs or face-to-face meetings. The more and more easily you interact with those around you, the stronger the friendship will be. All good ties rely on free, truthful contact.

We Have Great Relationships Human beings are inherently relational people—we want partnerships and meaningful experiences, much as we want food and water. It makes sense, then, that the stronger our relationships are at work, the happier and more successful we will be.

Healthy working relationships give us a range of other benefits: our job is more fun because we have a positive friendship with those around us. Often, people are more inclined to go along with the improvements that we want to make, so we become more ambitious so imaginative.

What's more, healthy relationships give us freedom: instead of wasting time and money to solve the challenges of bad relationships, we can now concentrate on rewards.

Good partnerships are also often needed if we want to grow our careers. After all, if the employer doesn't like you, it's doubtful that he or she will find you when a new role is opened. Overall, we all like to collaborate with people with whom we have a strong friendship.

We do require a strong working relationship with those in our professional community. Customers, vendors and core partners are all important to our progress. It is necessary, therefore, to establish and maintain good ties with these people.

How do you quantify the quality of your relationship with the individuals you deal with, like all human sciences, the quality of your relationship is easy to calculate, but very difficult to measure. You should assess your partnership, say stuff like "we're going great" or "we're the perfect fit!"But you're never going to hear anyone say," I love my wife and 8 out of 10!"You can't place a figure on it.

That said, it's better if you break it down into something concrete. When administrators are able to recognise aspects of their workers ' experience and team structures that require improvement, they are better prepared to take steps that can have a significant impact.

Technology has enabled us to recognize the key components that lead to employee engagement. Those include relations with our colleagues and with our superiors, and by posing detailed questions, we can better understand clearly which aspects of the interaction work well and others require more improvement.

In the end, interpersonal interactions are complicated. They take a lot of hard work and a lot of time to create. Yet when they are real, insightful, and significant, they carry our lives to a completely new level. In a world where technology is omnipresent, it is important for all of us to take a moment to slow down and interact with those around us, as it is with them that we share our lives, have meaningful encounters, create innovative goods or provide outstanding service.

When we engage in our organizational partnerships, we transition from individuals working together to a cohesive team that works together and communicates meaning.

Advisors

In our fast-paced, ever-changing business, we know that you're working hard. You aim to keep up with new technologies, applications, processes, and a constant flow of information while at the same time monitoring the day-to-day activities of your company. Yet there is one thing that remains a constant dream for all advisers: to become a trustworthy consultant.

Okay, what does that mean, how are you going to get there, and what are the future benefits?

Trusted Advisor Trust is described as "assured confidence in the integrity, capacity, power, or reality of someone or something." However, the word trustee has a fairly loose meaning in our industry. And (not surprisingly) boast that their clients are reliable advisors. But it's no easy challenge to get to this point. In order to better describe this, we need to take a closer look at where the company partnership starts.

Becoming a reliable partner means keeping the clients ' plans in place for the long term. Our free audit financial report guide will help.

Here are the various forms of company relationship:

Type 1. During the beginning of a partnership, certain clients can see you as a commodity seller or as someone who does one-off activities involving a certain technical competence. This is the point at which most consultants begin their careers, and it's the simplest form of master partnership. More essential, though, is where you can present yourself and then draw on your experience.

Type 2. At this point, the clients understand that you have expertise beyond the technological knowledge specific to the initial role you were hired to conduct. Using a few goods and resources, you will concentrate on addressing more general financial problems. Your customers, in effect, will continue to see you as a trustworthy tool and problem solver for more in-depth financial problems.

Type 3. Here, you are looked at in terms of your willingness to place things in detail and have insight. You give guidance and recognize customer problems as part of the operational process. At this moment, you can more quickly progress to the highest level within your relationship— that of a trusted counselor.

Type 4. When you have attained the level of trusted adviser, practically all issues— emotional or logical, personal or professional — are on the table for conversation and discovery. You should be the one the customer looks to as problems first arise— times of tremendous success, victory, loss, and crisis. This degree is also the most time-consuming, but often the most satisfying.

The Benefits of Being the Trusted Advisor

To make it transparent that you profit from repeat customers, as well as new recommendations and introductions of other qualified advisors to your clients. You don't need to "market" your goods or your experience while you're a trusted advisor. Instead, you should use the most respected skills you have— your capacity to learn, think, visualize, and proactively resolve client concerns. Here are just a few situations where your position as a trusted advisor will help both you and your clients.

Protecting senior clients: Your senior clients are the prime focus for financial harassment and, as their trusted lawyer, you will be their first line of protection. Bear in mind that 75 million people will be at least 65 years of age in 13 years, and that is sure to include plenty of the baby boomer customers. The accumulation of wealth in this community is enormous, and by developing a trusted relationship now, you will be better prepared to handle this wealth for future generations.

Keeping the Human Connection: We've all read of the emergence of the robo-advisor, and there's no question that it's a cost-effective technological solution. Yet as a trusted adviser, you give value to your customers in respects that robos obviously can not do. It involves, but is definitely not limited to, leveraging your expertise and instincts in risk analysis, handling your clients ' feelings in volatile business conditions, and delivering holistic strategic strategy around the financial planning continuum.

Developing your niche: Do you know that up to 70% of top financial consultants— defined as earning at least $1 million annually— have a niche? Developing a niche is, of course, a operation. Yet you will find that, over time, your reputation as a trustworthy adviser will not only help to improve your credibility, but will also help to develop you as an authority in your chosen field of expertise.

Internal development in the firm: for many contractors, growing up their company implies the possibility in obtaining a new profession. However, the importance of sustainable growth should not be ignored. One of the easiest ways to expand organically while preserving the quality of the company is to keep current clients happy by being their number one trusted partner. For satisfied and active customers, you will be on the road to improved funds and more referral possibilities.

What's up, huh?

First, have a look at where you're spending your time now and where you'd like to spend it in the future. Many business models are based on speed, performance, and a one-size-fits-all strategy, which also lacks the individual focus required to create trust. When you evaluate your client relationship, ask yourself the following questions to decide when you expend the most time and energy.

• Are you focused on the amount of consumers rather than quality? If so, you may like to consider doing the contrary.

• Have you built up a marketing plan? Setting down your expectations is a positive step in reaching them.

• Is your strength in building portfolios or building solid company relationships? Try selling the wealth services to allow more time to concentrate on partnerships.

• Should you waste precious time evaluating the expense of something instead of determining the importance of the programs provided to your customers and the practice? Note, cost is not the only thing that impacts the decision-making process.

The Road to Success How do you see the practice? When you want to concentrate solely on partnerships and trust, it will take time, commitment, and a lot of intellibence. But as you expand your company and pursue the professional partnership, placing yourself as a valued advisor is a simple road to success both now and in the future.

Keys To Improve The Relational Intelligence

Losing a job is one of the key worries of people today, according to a survey by the consultancy company NIELSEN, and while we know that there are external influences, such as inflation, the recession and unemployment, that are bringing an end to employment in the country, there is a cause that relies solely on you and the few people they are planning.

PEOPLE Get HIRED From Who You KNOW AND FIRED On Where That RELATES.

Typically, before someone is recruited for a particular job, the employer has gone to the point of ensuring that the candidate's studies and qualifications insure that they have the requisite academic skills, but perhaps the most challenging problems we encounter in professional life have to do with our interpersonal relationships. Difficulty in recognizing certain forms of thought, functioning or communicating has become the source of tension for professionals. In reality, we are all persuaded that there are three types of people for work: those who do, those who know what to do, and those who encourage us to think and behave in exceptional ways. Obviously, the last ones are the most difficult to locate, and that's why they've always had JOB OFFERS.

Relationship intelligence is a ability that you can't lack in your toolkit to create an outstanding life, here I share some strategies to improve your IQ Relational:• Establish Emotional Intelligence: Usually, it's not behaviors, but our perceptions of the behaviors of others that bug us. The creation of this other intellect helps you to see things differently. Know, the best possible understanding of a scenario is usually the one that holds you in an mental state that encourages the realization of your dreams, and the wrong understanding is the one that brings you to a state that sabotages your dreams.

• Don't take things personally: we want to think that something is political, because if anyone doesn't welcome me, it's because he thinks more than me, or that if he criticizes me, it's because he has something toward me. We encourage you to relax and internally say, "I can see this differently," when someone has an awkward situation.

• Acknowledge the pain of others: No one gets up and begs God to "Allow me to be ill-tempered" or "I want you to give me a day of complaints and resentment." Talk about how many days you slip into your key fault (whatever it is) and remember that even though it hurts you and affects your future, you do it not for fun but because you lack control of the situation. No one is furious, cynical, arrogant, insecure, dangerous, hostile, greedy, or something for fun, just just at some point we run out of internal energy to be content, which is what we all really want.

• Meditate daily: meditation is an excellent way to learn to improve emotional maturity and to be less sensitive. When you don't have training, the only way you can do to learn is to use guided meditation to help you control your mind and not wind up with your eyes closed worrying about who knows what or sleeping on your couch. Practice is the important thing!

Relational Intelligence skills to create communication relationships

Building enriching relationships is for me a maxim in life, Relational Intelligence is part of creativity and without cultivating the first, it is difficult to make our talents grow and shine. Mentors and coaches build learning and development partnerships that enable talent to flourish and evolve. There you can see the Relational Intelligence Skills, which are used to build relationships of interaction.

1.-Practical silence: learning how to be quiet, how to stop speaking, not interrupting, not having to occupy the gap created by silence.

To follow in silence is to abandon oneself in the arms of the other and to forget my pride, my desire to fulfill a sense of worth, to decide, to instruct, to show my considerable intellibence and experience, or my need for acknowledgment.

Not leaving room for silence prevents others from being able to reveal their internal states and explore them in order to increase their self-knowledge and understanding.

2.-Welcoming: Silence in combination with global and deep listening helps to actively and warmly welcome, understand and accept the ideas and models of others, their emotions, reactions, affirmations, doubts as they are. Welcoming means not evaluating, not judging, it's not about agreeing or disagreeing or comparing, it's just receiving and welcoming what the others share with us.

Welcoming the body, the soul, the heart and the mind, welcoming the others with all our bcing, offering them the space of trust and openness that they need to explore their potential

3.-Looking: The eye, along with an relaxed stance, is the most important tool for embracing, building confidence, promoting transparency and connection in a partnership. Four minutes of touching eyes create more intimacy in relationships, and that has unexpected results.

People immediately note every change in eye contact that causes a change in interaction, and potentially a break in the relationship. Much of the breaks in the look come from our inner conversation as it surprises us, takes our focus, and diverts it from the other's eye. We're no longer with him, we're no longer talking to him, we're engaged in an infinite argument with our ego.

4.-Accompaniment, verbally andnon-verbally, by an assent through a head or a look, a grin, or by sounds or phrases. Nodding instinctively in line with the words of everyone else means that we are present to him and that we embrace him. Can we also assist him with verbal phrases such as "how cool, start" or interjections such as eh, eh, yeah, yeah, wow, really? Y? Yeah, huh? etc., you're going to get much more attended.

Even if, without going over, without encroaching upon their habitat, we have to take into account whether they are an extrovert, who require more constant representations of presence, or an introvert, who appear to be very relaxed with less presence and interference.

Another very successful method of verbal accompaniment is to echo the last word or the most important or meaningful words of the other, which turns conversation into a true synchronized dance.

5. —Positive affirmation reinforces the individual, encourages them to continue, motivates them to continue. Quotes like "Nice job," "Perfect job," "I applaud you for all your success and the outcomes obtained" or "I appreciate your drive to succeed,"

"What a brilliant idea," "How fascinating," keep the connection intact, linked and reinforced with the client, given they are honest and timely. 6.-Validate: grant the client permission to acknowledge their own truth, feelings, opinions, thoughts."Is there a question I can ask you?"Can I share my feeling with you right now?"I would like to tell you what I think about myself. You let me do that?"Ask for permission is a sign of appreciation for the other that strengthens the relationship. Also, asking for permission brings emphasis on what has to be discussed and that makes the discussion even more dynamic. 9.-Invite: another quality that demonstrates empathy and reverence for the other is encouraging him to discuss, to offer his view, to add his idea, etc."It's an open opportunity for the customer to continue communicating." I encourage you to focus on that in the following mechanisms... that may be a means of implying that the client considers different forms of focusing toward their target or circumstance. 10.-Undressing: that empathic skill consists in expressing our emotions with the client, or our most intimate encounters, at moments when the client wants a grea. Will you want to see her?

All of us who assist others will embrace and appreciate our weakness, and in addition to making us embrace that of others, recognizing it and allowing them to reconnect with it, it would serve us to humbly acknowledge our shortcomings and share them with the customer, without guilt, if possible. Expression of strong emotion or a uncomfortable situation that occurs in a session may help to improve the interaction, maintain the required state to proceed, and provide the individual with an indication of emotional control.

Undressing often means risking sharing our assumptions and intuitions with the customer on what he is asking us to help him become aware of something that has slipped his mind. Sharing them means believing that they are their own and the probability that they are incorrect, because they must always be verified by the client 11.-Reform: it consistsof re-expressing in their own terms a complicated or comprehensive concept formed by the client and, then, questioning him about the consistency of the response. A strong reformulation conveys to the other that we listen to him with complete care, that we hear him and that we are there with all our energy to help him. Any reformulation must be approved by him, out of reverence for the other.

Reformulation often acts as a mirror of the individual, placing their thoughts and expressions before them and being able to consider them at a distance.

12.-Assuming what is your own and not appropriating what belongs to others: as we talk, we have to do so on our own, believing our thoughts, intuitions, reformulations, etc., and not attributing them to the customer, to another person, or not understanding who (the popular« they tell», the people...). We must also send back to the client all his actions, his successes and his duties, which are not necessary. Expressions such as "I might be incorrect but...," "I'm not aware of your comment but...," "I don't know whether I heard you right but...," "I'm not aware whether I understand you but...," "This could be an understanding of mine but...," etc., are several examples of adding a point of view, a reformulation or a hypothesis, but at the same time offering the individual the ability to deny it, acknowledge and agree whether our point of view is.

Chapter Three

Discernment and Balance in Relationships

When you learn a lesson in love from an advanced mind, you're up and going! You find it easy to care about others; you open your heart and let love spill out; you do all you can to make people feel good; you dedicate yourself to giving, caring and helping; and you do your best to be unconditional. So then you're going to collapse flat on your stomach and have a mental break down! Yeah, ha ha. For everything that you have given, you have failed to keep a balance in your life, and you have been so busy worrying about others that you have not been able to care of yourself—your energy; your physical needs and your own emotional needs.

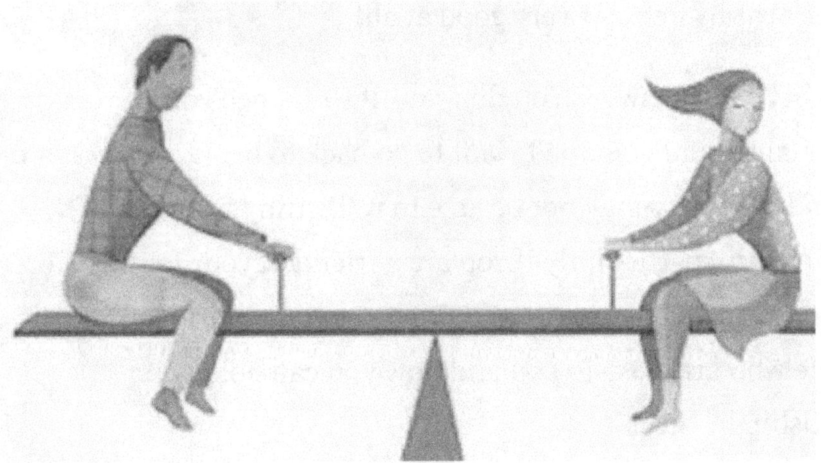

It's a pit that passes through every caring and open-minded soul I know of.

If we give to people who are grateful and who give back love and gratitude, it's simple. These people make you feel comfortable in every way, and probably all of your nearest friends and relatives will fall into this group. So if you have someone that doesn't–someone who is hesitant to pick up a phone or start a messaging conversation or who is more self-interest-oriented than you or other people, then the friendship could be out of control.

Because of their obvious disapproval of your goodness, you may find that you get upset and resentful, which in effect makes you feel bad, and then you beat yourself up because you're trying your best to remain caring and compassionate, because you don't want to feel such destructive unpleasant feelings. And what started out as a flow of love will turn into a flow of vitriol! Never healthy and not very good at all!

So, what's the answer? You don't want to change your personality, and you don't want to go back to being reckless and unkind. You may may not be able to walk away from this relationship, particularly if you are a friend of your family. Here are a few tips to make sure you don't get your heart broken by people who are close to you and how you can hold your friendship in check.

• Drop your expectations from this guy. Most of the pain stems from unfulfilled aspirations, and we sometimes place them too high on those that are close to us. Not everybody is willing to offer unconditionally, and certain people have characteristics of character that can be annoying or disturbing. You may have set the bar too high for this guy.

• If your friend doesn't act like you want a friend to act, then re-categorize them; take them out of a box of friends, and place them in a box of friends! Then your needs will be smaller, you'll waste less time on them, and you won't feel the need to give too much, so you'll probably expect less.

• Control your behavior and attitudes towards your colleagues. Note that if you go too hard and give too much, you will put the other person on the spot—they do not have the same money or time as you do, and they may begin to feel bad. It is going to help them back off and throw the partnership out of control again.

• Taking a look back from here. When someone upsets you with their behaviour and attitude towards you, so take a step back, cover your emotions with a shield of thick walls and hide when they get furious with you—when you know they're going through a difficult time, don't take what they mean seriously, because they're just venting their own bad thoughts to the one that's closest to them.

• If the person that has offended you is a friend of the family, imagine them in a golden bubble—a Perspex dome that holds a lovely spot for them—I use a field full of flowers in the light. Give them love, so keep your distance as much as you can, but be open to getting them back when they're able to treat you again.

Get rid of your own disappointment induced by other people's behaviour. Write down everything you know and burn it out. Now that the tears are streaming into Earth to be recycled!

• Put yourself on the list of those you want to be loved and caring for. Please, not the bottom of the page!

Finally, be discerning with the preference of mates and partners everywhere you can. Always, be discerning about what you're doing with people who don't accept your goodness.

Signs Of A healthy Relationship

You can, of course, grow happier when you become a stronger version of yourself. However, this is not the joy that comes from someone finding you amazing or sending you the best presents. The pleasure you feel is the comfort and joy of realizing that you are becoming more like yourself.

It's easy to be happy when someone else uses your love language. Even the wrong companion will speak your language for a while and make you feel good. However, feeling good is not the aim of a stable relationship, and these moments won't tell you whether or not you're in a healthy relationship. Don't get me wrong, you deserve to get positive feelings.

Nonetheless, this requirement is somewhat different from the intent of a partnership. To know if a relationship is safe, we need to examine how we respond when we don't have the consolation of gifts or the expressions of affirmation or love and affection.

There are a lot of considerations that will help you cope with your partner's loss of affection, such as previous encounters or wounds, your hopes, or your potential for weakness. It may also be affected by what you really see in the other guy. You might be holding on for comfort, but when it comes down to it, you don't really want the other guy, and your lack of stability or desire to flourish in times of desolation shows how you truly feel about the relationship. No matter what the cause, though, how you continue to get through tough periods with your significant others can tell you how safe the relationship is. Here are a few indicators that prove you are in a stable relationship 1. Mutual integrity shall be upheld.

Only two people who respect each other's integrity will build a healthy partnership. Good regard for the integrity of another person means that you treat the other person as the sort of being who appears for his or her own benefit, not merely to satisfy your needs or to be used as an object. In a stable relationship, you view the other individual as being created for his or her own benefit, with a history and a story that is entirely special and valuable purely by being his or her own. If you're already dating, you understand that this story can or may not have you in the long run. When you are married, you know that your vows are the key to the fulfillment of your existence as well as that of your partner.

This can be very quick to adopt a selfish attitude towards another person in a relationship. I don't assume that you're consciously talking about using a person, but your attitudes, emotions, and feelings that begin to suggest an inner attitude that the other person exists for your gain or advantage in this relationship. This agreement would easily destroy the relationship. At all, it would be a shared usage relationship of fixed conditions for a while before it fully dissolves into something unstable.

If you value the integrity of the other party, you ask yourself, "What is really right for him or her?"You know, too, that he or she is asking about you. You may also want the other to inquire for you — not that you want the positive for yourself— but you know the when he or she poses the question for you, it's the way to become the best possible self.

2. Second, you try fellowship.

In my experience, one of the most important indicators of a stable relationship is to have a good bond in the middle of romance. Friendship is the sort of partnership that can survive any wind, as well as the changing seasons in other relationships. Physical attraction, temperament matching, and interest continuity are all essential facets of a relationship, but intimacy alone will take a relationship over the years. A easy way to think about friendship is to imagine taking a cross-country road trip with the person in question.

A good relationship is one where two people will enjoy a journey together, with all the fun and often unpleasant encounters that may come with it. Marriage has been going on for a long time, so most secondary characteristics will either pass on or change, but friendship will take a few to the end.

3. There is interdependence, not liberty or dependency.

There's a lot of psycho-talk these days about expectations and preserving your freedom. It's a core component of emotional and spiritual maturity, but it's just part of the scene. In the same time, we are made for the world (at the end, to be part of the fellowship of the saints), and so we begin now with the way we communicate with others.

There is an acceptable amount of attachment that goes along with each form of relationship, but essentially marriage is the one that requires a complete gift of self to the other. This truth involves the ambiguity of preserving your own identity and, at the same time, establishing a new form of identification as a married couple. There is a feeling of relation that is necessary beyond independence; this is what we call interdependence. A stable relationship is one in which there is a tension between people's individual personalities and deep affection and closeness to each other.

4. The partnership is founded on confidence.

If the relationship is based on intimacy, as described above, then trust is obviously included. This means that you will share your secrets with your partner; you know that he or she can respect your honesty, and you will give the same. There is no question of deception, cheating or, in any way, of knowingly harming the other person. You feel free to talk about anything: your pains, your worries, your wishes or your dreams. You're free to play on your own.

5. You should assist each other in difficult moments, but you do know when you need outside assistance.

These points can show flaws in your relationship. An unhealthful relationship doesn't automatically mean it's going to end. When a promise is made, it surely can't stop. We're going to work on our vulnerabilities for the remainder of our lives, and there's bound to be moments when we're unsafe towards our mate and moments when he or she's unsafe towards us. It's nice to learn that sometimes it's Safe to ask for support.

You should go to your family, trusted friends, a spiritual assistant, or even a psychiatrist to get through harder things. Often when dating there is an inevitable discovery that a relationship really isn't going to work for two parties, often in marriage there is a recognition that marital therapy is needed to develop. Underlying both of these facets of a good partnership is a maturity that helps a person to know when to assist each other emotionally and when to venture beyond the help partnership.

Acceptance Of Your Relationship

It is often said that joy comes from the approval of our partnership. And everyone would agree that acceptance is important in marriages, but the real question is: how do we get to the position of deeper acceptance in our relationship? This is a very difficult subject. For others, recognition may be a process over time, while for others it may be a little simpler. Here are my thoughts on this difficult topic.

Start with you: while it is natural to concentrate instinctively on the harm that our partner brings to us, it can be difficult and daunting to acknowledge the damage that our partner creates. One part of the road to profound understanding of your relationship is to accept the obstacles that you bring to it. It's hard to accept the obstacles your partner brings to your relationship without acknowledging your own obstacles. I admit, this is a difficult one. Self-acceptance is self-love and self-compassion. It doesn't mean you're fine. It means that you embrace the obstacles that you bring to your relationship and, better yet, continue to focus on self-awareness and personal development. Keep that in mind, when you step towards self-acceptance, you come out of anxiety, guilt, and other debilitating feelings. What a beautiful present!

All of us have emotional triggers: knowing the emotional triggers of our partner (with compassion) will help you progress towards greater recognition of your spouse and your partnership. For eg, one may have a strong reaction when one is attacked (due to intense childhood rejection, this becomes an emotional trigger) and one's spouse may have a fear of abandonment (due to being rejected in childhood by a parent, this becomes an emotional trigger). No one in their life escapes the feeling of suffering, no one. You may have had the best parents in the world, but even the best parents are unwittingly causing pain. And nobody avoids suffering in other life experiences, whether they're going to happen at school, in a relationship, or in a stressful encounter. In our new relationship, past wounds are always magnified. Past wounds are caused when our companion (often unknowingly) strikes them.

In a couple of my blogs, I've talked about emotional causes. It's really important to consider them in your partner and yourself. It is important to strike a compromise between being mindful of the triggers of each other and not taking blame for the triggers of your partner. For example, if your partner has an emotional reason to be insulted, you should focus on how you address your partner's complaints. You wouldn't say, "You're lazy and don't do much around the house," but then, "I'm exhausted by everything that I have to do. Should we think about how we can help each other out? (Side note, even because you're expressing your question to your partner in the best way imaginable, it doesn't guarantee that they'll react positively to you.) But it can be the beginning of a dialogue. Not doing something to your friend, since they are upset by abuse, is simply taking responsibility for them. We also have to handle our own causes, and we are responsible for them. As friends, we can only work to stop perpetuating the suffering in each other's causes.

Bear in mind, the more we grasp each other's emotional stimuli, the more we can communicate with each other in an appropriate and respectful way.

Be vigilant of the guidance of others: we all need a support net. This is priceless. And still, the guidance we seek from others always comes from one location or another. One, they love you, and they don't want to see you harmed. As a consequence, guidance is always offered from a position of compassion, and yet it is not necessarily a path to acceptance. For example, someone may say to you, "You don't need that kind of action from your partner," and while that might be accurate, it's not beneficial (unless you actually want to end the relationship) because what you really need is a clarification of what you're going through AND a path forward. A way forward also means supplying both of you with understanding. Receiving support just for you can make it all the more difficult to embrace your partner and your friendship.

Second, advice also comes from the perspective of the person giving you advice. Here's the thing: what you embrace in a relationship may not be reasonable to others, and that's all right.

Every of us is distinctly special, dependent on so many factors, our personality, life experiences, childhood, and so on. Each of us will embrace things about our spouse and our partnership that others will not consider. And again, that's all right!

Advice from others may confuse you. It will make you challenge yourself in unhelpful ways and give rise to doubts. Relationships are difficult and hard work, indeed. It is easier to step towards acceptance in your relationship if you receive advice from someone who can provide both of you with empathy and encouragement.

Expectations, limits and forgiveness: there are not those of us who are completely prepared for the work of dedicated partnerships. We will have hopes, aspirations, and anticipation for the future together. We never consider the amount of grace that we're going to have to apply. The challenging thing about redemption is that we don't realize how bad we've been hurt. This is where it is necessary to recognize the shortcomings of you and your partner. What I mean by that is to understand (and accept) that your partner (or you) will not be everything you expect in a relationship. For example, your husband may be genuinely sorry for upsetting you, but he may not know how to convey remorse emotionally to the degree that it will help serve your needs. Adjusting our standards and awareness of one's shortcomings will get you closer to acceptance in your relationship. And, of course, it's going to bring you back to redemption.

Acceptance does not mean that you comply with all actions of your mate. The only thing you can do with a behaviour that you don't agree with in your relationship is to decide whether you want to react. It's more inspiring than it seems. Knowing how you can react to what you don't agree with is something you can control, but it's not supposed to be used against your partner. For example, if your partner makes false claims, you might opt to disengage from this relationship with your partner. Let them know that you'd like to have a discussion without costs, and that you're ready to do it when they're done. Or if your partner withdraws from you for whatever reason, it's time for self-care and self-care, or having a nice time doing stuff that you love before your partner is able to reconnect in a way that meets all of your needs.

Acceptance doesn't mean you're going to stop focusing on personal development. Acceptance does not mean that you believe that "he / she will never improve" in a pessimistic state of mind. I know this may appear to contradict the concept of approval, but what it means is that you still stay open to potential personal development in your partner.

Acceptance does not mean that you tolerate abusive care, such as physical abuse or other serious aggressive behaviour. I use the term "serious" because I've seen people use the term "violence" a little too quickly. Let's hope you know what I mean by the word "violence."

Acceptance is not about' giving up' or' giving in,' it's about understanding that you're in your friendship right now.

Acceptance is recognizing the difficulties, mental causes, and fragility between you and your family. It's knowing that all of you aren't flawless, so sometimes you get hurt. Acceptance is realizing that your mate is unlikely to satisfy any of your desires. Acceptance is letting go of what your friend would "wish" for you. And let me promise that, in the end, tolerance will be freeing for you both. And who knows what recognition is going to do to your friendship. Acceptance is a very important thing!

Aligning your relationship

Compatibility ensures that you are working and caring in the same way as someone else. If you don't take the time and energy to match your dream, fundamental principles, and desires with your partner, the partnership will eventually begin to pay off.

Relationships will never be uncomfortable to remember. If you feel like you need to be someone else to fulfill your partner's expectations, or if you struggle too hard that you're depressed and upset all the time, it's time to reconsider your friendship with someone else.

Life is too small to do so.

Love is intended to lift you up and inspire you to become a better version of yourself. When you're partnered with your friend, there's an agreement between the two of you that you're going in the same direction. If that doesn't happen, both men are wasting their time.

Achieving relationship harmony starts by learning and accepting what the main relationship principles are. That's how we get insight on the type of person we want to share our lives with.

In her novel, Atlas Shrugged, Ayn Rand says, "Joy is our answer to our highest values— and nothing else can be. Our passion for ourselves is embodied in all that we do and all that we want to have in our lives. And the most personal of our relationships teach us the most about how we care of ourselves and what we want. "Sometimes people feel too happy in a relationship, or worse, they feel lost in it. They end up losing their fundamental beliefs, which contribute to frustration and anger.

Let's discuss three things you can do to feel better compatible with your mate.

2. Know What The Love Language Is A Love Language is a language that we use as we show it. How are you going to wake up and give love to your partner? If you don't know what you or your partner's love language is, I recommend you to read Dr.

Gary Chapman's book The Five Love Languages: The Guide to Marriage That Lasts. In his novel, he says that complications will emerge when your love language doesn't suit your partner's.

In order to be compatible, you don't have to use the same love language as your mate. It is critical, however, that you understand and respect what their language is. Communication is the secret to the sustainability of each partnership. We just deserve to be heard at the end of the day.

2. Show Sympathy For Times When They Seem Out Of Sync We all have poor days where we feel out of balance. When this happens, we will also impose our insecurities and fears to our friends. I agree that empathy and kindness will always come before guidance when it comes to relationships.

Nobody likes to be preached when they feel weak, particularly when they're loving. According to a recent research published in Sentiment, love is the most essential characteristic of a successful marriage.

My girlfriend and I love one another unconditionally. Often our behaviour reveals something different, particularly when we're depressed or distracted by work. We never take it seriously, though. When you go through issues with your friend, you also need to be mindful of your own ego.

It's about learning how to keep your partner's room when they're unable to do so on their own. This is the purest type of unconditional love that will allow you and your partner to develop together. No one is fine.

When you embrace this and show respect for someone else's emotions, it encourages more open dialogue and intimacy to take place in your relationship.

3. Have an Consensus on Your Dream, Ideals and Fundamental Convictions Our principles form our lives; they determine how we act, the choices we make and, ultimately, the people with which we associate ourselves. When you're going against your principles, every fibre of your being realizes that you have it. You just end up feeling sad and unfulfilled. This is not the way to live.

If your dream in life is to be an Internet entrepreneur and wander the globe, but your partner's goal is to become a lawyer, purchase a home, and live in one location, you will ultimately follow two different dreams. This example illustrates a simple misalignment of beliefs between two individuals.

When it comes to your most valuable principles, you need to evolve in the same direction as your partner. In the words of Abraham Hicks, "When you reach balance, the circumstances won't matter." Partnership harmony is the cornerstone of long-term success and satisfaction.

Do the groundwork to make sure you know what's important to you as a partner, and then engage in an honest conversation with someone at the beginning of your relationship. Tell your lover what you need and make sure you know what they need.

Understanding how your values are aligned or not aligned with someone will allow you to build a healthy and long-lasting relationship with them, or encourage you to move on and find someone who shares the same values as you do.

Assessing Your Relationships

There is one maxim when it comes to dating and marriages that I truly believe in, and it is never to be resolved. You deserve a lot more than that. We're all deserving of great love and fireworks!

"Don't stop" doesn't mean adopting the shallow checklist you made when you were 16, where the emphasis is on hair color, precise height, profession, salary, etc. Not going to compromise is just about how somebody makes you feel. Do you feel content, safe, loved, appreciated?

The fact that you're challenging your relationship says a lot about yourself; choosing to move on or to call it a stop will weigh heavily on your heart and mind. We should be trusted only as much as we respect ourselves.

HERE ARE SEVEN QUESTIONS TO CONSIDER WHILE EVALUATING YOUR RELATIONSHIP:

1. Do they make you happy?

Do you look forward to your time together? Are you excited about them? Are you inquisitive to continue to learn more about them and what makes them tick? As we settle into relationships it's normal for that initial over-the-moon excitement to diminish slightly, but you should still be looking forward to spending time together .

Philosopher Joseph Campbell stated, "follow your bliss". If your partner is not representing "bliss" for you then that's a definite red light.

2. Do you share the same values?

Do you both value family, honesty, loyalty, friends, career, philanthropy, communication, intimacy, etc? They say opposites attract, and that's fine and dandy as far as hobbies, interests and even personalities go to an extent. You should still share some of the above because you want a partner to experience life and create memories with.

Values are a different story; values are your "rules of life". They are a fundamental part of who you are and are generally consistent throughout life; you've probably had a similar set of values since childhood. Your values directly influence who you interact with, how you respond to situations and the choices you make in life. If someone doesn't share the same values, then arguments and frustrations are a guarantee.

3. Do you trust your partner?

Is your partner honest, reliable and faithful? Trust is the foundation for building a strong relationship. Trust means that you expect integrity, respect, and loyalty to be at the center of your relationship, and that you have placed your faith and your confidence in your partner. You expect your partner to keep promises and to stick it out when the going gets tough. Trust is earned over time as you get to know your partner more intimately and isn't something to give lightly. Hopefully if you are still spending time with this person, then you have established they are worthy of your trust. If not, then the relationship needs to be re-evaluated.

4. Can you be yourself?

Most of us can pretend to be people we are not. We do this in hopes of gaining approval from others. Do you act out of character when with your partner? Doing so is exhausting and cannot be sustained long-term, you are simply wasting your time and the time of your partner. Don't violate your identity because you think someone will like you better. The world needs YOU. There is nothing sexier then authenticity. There really is a lid for every pot so be yourself so that the partner you are supposed to be with will recognize you.

5. Does your partner bring you up or bring you down?

Are you happy more than you are sad? There are always going to be bumps in the road in every relationship. Feelings are going to get hurt. People are going to make mistakes and be unfair at times. These times however should be few and far in-between. It's amazing how many people cry every day and still wonder if the relationship is the right one for them. Life is short. You deserve happiness, and the great news is that it's simply a choice. Have the courage to leave any situation that is not creating happiness in your life. You must get rid of what no longer serves you to make room for what will.

6. Can you communicate?

The best relationships have amazing communication. No one is a mind reader. If you desire something, say it. If something bothers you, tell your partner. It's really not what you say, it's HOW you say. Speak with love and compassion. Do not attack. Be a solution finder.

7. Are they interested in Personal Growth?

This is not some new age babble, it's a fact. Many relationships end because one person outgrew the other or in other cases one person's core beliefs were sabotaging the relationship. All relationships begin with self. We must consistently excavate. Dig deep below the surface, look at our shadows and work on ourselves. Relationships serve as our greatest spiritual teachers because they often trigger in us what needs to be healed, but we must we willing to do the work. It takes 2 to tango! One person cannot carry the whole relationship, both parties must be equally invested in personal growth for the relationship to flourish and sustain long term.

It can be scary to leave a situation in fear that you will not ever find anyone else, but you will. Stay true to yourself, continue working on yourself and you will attract the right person for you. It can also be scary to surrender to a relationship. Perhaps you are looking for reasons as to why this relationship won't work because you are scared to get hurt. Perhaps your core beliefs are that you are not good enough, or don't deserve a great relationship so you sabotage it before you get too involved. There is no better feeling than to love and to be loved. It is our birthright.

True friends share our lives: the good times and the bad. Our friends can be more or less close, and more or less loyal, and our relationships with them depend a lot on what we expect from friendship in general.

I consider myself to be a person with lots of friends. But are they close friends? Not necessarily, but they are all "good" friends. And by that I mean I am happy to have them all in my life. I've put them into five categories, and I think we all fall into one of these categories in somebody's life.

The "Friendish" Friend

These are friends that are on the surface friends. Most of my work friends fall into this category. Chances are we've never been to each other's houses, we don't go out socially, but we hang out at work, like each other, and know a bit about each other's lives. I like my "friendish" friends, and don't really find the need to make it a deeper friendship.

The "Fair Weather" Friend

A lot of people have heard of fair weather friends. A lot of people consider this to be a bad thing. These are friend that you may hang out with or socialize with sometimes, and maybe you have even been to each other's houses. But when a crisis occurs they keep their distance. I'm actually okay with that. If I or someone I love is going through something, I don't need the whole world to know. I'd rather be surrounded by those closest to me.

The "Foul Weather" Friend

This is the opposite of "fair weather" friends. You may not see them or be in touch with them as often as you'd like, but in a crisis they're right there for you, asking what they can do to help. I think I am this kind of friend to a lot of people. I'm bad at keeping in touch, but I promise if you need me, I'll be there.

The "Forever" Friend

This is the person that you have know forever, but hardly ever see or talk to them. Yet, when you do it's like no time has passed. You will always have a connection, you love this person, and you're both okay with your lack of correspondence. Even though you promise each other that you'll be in touch sooner next time.

The "Family" Friend

These are the people that are so close that you consider them family. You talk to them all the time, you see them on weekends and even during the week. They know everything about you, and you would do anything for each other. I'm happy to say I have a nice little circle of friends I call "family" friends. I love them and would be lost without them.

Establishing and developing good friendships can be one of the most important and rewarding areas of our lives, yet it is one that many clients find difficult and wish to work on.

Eliciting client beliefs and self-defeating thoughts is an important part of the process. However, some clients may never have learned how to form healthy relationships.

Literature strongly supports a direct and positive relationship between the quality of persons' friendships and his or her health. Thus, the ability to make and sustain fulfilling friendships has a great effect on both emotional as well as physical well-being. Learning more about the nature of friendships enables clients improve this area of their lives.

A friendship model

To help our clients create and develop enduring, good quality friendships, we introduce them to a simple model, The Circle of Friendship and Intimacy. You can talk through the model with your client, helping them see developing friendships as a journey that passes through several stages. Explain to the client that various "Key Factors" will help the friendship develop healthily.

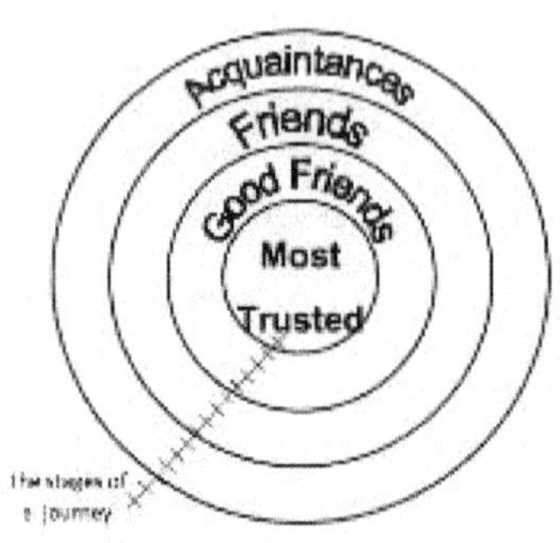

The key factors the client should be aware of being:

1. Trust.

Trust develops over a period of time. Placing trust in people too quickly may lead to disappointments. For acquaintances to become friends, trust needs to be solidly established.

2. Protection.

At the start of a relationship we may be naturally reserved in order to avoid hurt and disappointment. This is an important factor as it prevents us from "rushing in", rather than taking time to develop the friendship at a sensible pace. For example, people who disclose too much too soon can put others off. However, it can also inhibit the development of trust, as we can project our lack of trust on to others, and it becomes a self-fulfilling prophecy. The balance is important.

3. Risk.

Overly protecting ourselves emotionally can prevent people from getting close to us, as we give so little to the relationship in terms of revealing ourselves. This prevents the relationship from developing. We also need to accept warmth from others. We need to take some emotional risks, and share more about ourselves in order to move through the circles of friendship. Clients working in corporate settings will be very familiar with the terms, Risk Assessment and Risk Management.

4. Testing the water.

This helps us to assess and manage the risks by asking ourselves questions such as:

"Do we really get on that well?"

"What do we have in common?"

"Is this friendship worth developing?"

"Do I feel confident and happy spending time with this person?"

Time can be spent re-evaluating how we see the friendship going and whether we really wish to move forward with it.

5. Emotional Decision Making.

As we discover the areas in which we are alike and different from others, we can assess whether the friendship meets our needs effectively or not. This involves us in emotional decision-making. We can do this at any point in the Circle of Friendship, and need to ask ourselves whether we really wish to move forward with a particular friendship, or whether we should consider limiting or terminating it – i.e. leaving it in one of the outer circles of the model.

As the client becomes familiar with the model, he or she will begin to understand one of the most important aspects of all good relationships – pacing.

6. Pacing.

In this context refers to our ability to keep pace emotionally with another person, as the relationship moves through various stages. We are free to set the pace ourselves, or follow the pace of our friend; the important point is that we are flexible enough to move either forwards or backwards to keep ourselves in the same part of the circle that they are in, and to move on together, as trust and intimacy increases.

A Written Exercise

In order to discover how to improve or increase his friendship circle, the client can start by asking himself the following questions about his current and past friendships.

Do I feel that...

- I give more than I get in friendships

- My confidence and trust is abused

- My friends are not really 'there for me' when I need them

- I do most of the compromising with my friends

Answering "yes" to any of these questions suggests that the balance between the "give and take" elements of the friendship has gone awry, and/or that the client may want more (or less) from the friendship than is realistic.

Chapter Four

Habits of People Who Build Extraordinary Relationships

The most extraordinary professional relationships are built by ordinary actions like these. Professional success is important to everyone, but still, success in business and in life means different things to different people--as well it should.

But one fact is universal: Real success, the kind that exists on multiple levels, is impossible without building great relationships. Real success is impossible unless you treat other people with kindness, regard, and respect.

After all, you can be a rich jerk... but you will also be a lonely jerk.

That's why people who build extraordinary business relationships:

1. Take the hit.

A customer gets mad. A vendor complains about poor service. A mutual friend feels slighted.

Sometimes, whatever the issue and regardless of who is actually at fault, some people step in and take the hit. They're willing to accept the criticism or abuse because they know they can handle it--and they know that maybe, just maybe, the other person can't.

Few acts are more selfless than taking the undeserved hit. And few acts better cement a relationship.

2. Step in without being asked.

It's easy to help when you're asked. Most people will.

Very few people offer help before they have been asked, even though most of the time that is when a little help will make the greatest impact.

People who build extraordinary relationships pay close attention so they can tell when others are struggling. Then they offer to help, but not in a general, "Is there something I can do to help you?" way.

Instead they come up with specific ways they can help. That way they can push past the reflexive, "No, I'm okay..." objections. And they can roll up their sleeves and make a difference in another person's life.

Not because they want to build a better relationship, although that is certainly the result, but simply because they care.

3. Answer the question that is not asked.

Where relationships are concerned, face value is usually without value. Often people will ask a different question than the one they really want answered.

A colleague might ask you whether he should teach a class at a local college; what he really wants to talk about is how to take his life in a different direction.

A partner might ask how you felt about the idea he presented during the last board meeting; what he really wants to talk about is his diminished role in the running of the company.

An employee might ask how you built a successful business; instead of kissing up he might be looking for some advice--and encouragement--to help him follow his own dreams.

Behind many simple questions is often a larger question that goes unasked. People who build great relationships think about what lies underneath so they can answer that question, too.

4. Know when to dial it back.

Outgoing and charismatic people are usually a lot of fun... until they aren't. When a major challenge pops up or a situation gets stressful, still, some people can't stop "expressing their individuality." (Admit it: You know at least one person so in love with his personality he can never dial it back.)

People who build great relationships know when to have fun and when to be serious, when to be over the top and when to be invisible, and when to take charge and when to follow.

Great relationships are multifaceted and therefore require multifaceted people willing to adapt to the situation--and to the people in that situation.

5. Prove they think of others.

People who build great relationships don't just think about other people. They act on those thoughts.

One easy way is to give unexpected praise. Everyone loves unexpected praise--it's like getting flowers not because it's Valentine's Day, but "just because." Praise helps others feel better about themselves and lets them know you're thinking about them (which, if you think about it, is flattering in itself.)

Take a little time every day to do something nice for someone you know, not because you're expected to but simply because you can. When you do, your relationships improve dramatically.

6. Realize when they have acted poorly.

Most people apologize when their actions or words are called into question.

Very few people apologize before they are asked to--or even before anyone notices they should.

Responsibility is a key building block of a great relationship. People who take the blame, who say they are sorry and explain why they are sorry, who don't try to push any of the blame back on the other person--those are people everyone wants in their lives, because they instantly turn a mistake into a bump in the road rather than a permanent roadblock.

7. Give consistently, receive occasionally.

A great relationship is mutually beneficial. In business terms that means connecting with people who can be mentors, who can share information, who can help create other connections; in short, that means going into a relationship wanting something.

The person who builds great relationships doesn't think about what she wants; she starts by thinking about what she can give.

She sees giving as the best way to establish a real relationship and a lasting connection. She approaches building relationships as if it's all about the other person and not about her, and in the process builds relationships with people who follow the same approach.

In time they make real connections.

And in time they make real friends.

8. Value the message by always valuing the messenger.

When someone speaks from a position of position of power or authority or fame it's tempting to place greater emphasis on their input, advice, and ideas.

We listen to Tony Hsieh. We listen to Norm Brodsky. We listen to Seth Godin.

The guy who mows our lawn? Maybe we don't listen to him so much.

That's unfortunate. Smart people strip away the framing that comes with the source--whether positive or negative--and consider the information, advice, or idea based solely on its merits.

People who build great relationships never automatically discount the message simply because they discount the messenger. They know good advice is good advice, regardless of where it comes from.

And they know good people are good people, regardless of their perceived "status."

9. Start small… and are happy to stay small.

I sometimes wear a Reading Football Club sweatshirt. The checkout clerk at the grocery store noticed it one day and said, "Oh, you're a Reading supporter? My team is Manchester United."

Normally, since I'm pretty shy, I would have just nodded and said something innocuous, but for some reason I said, "You think Man U can beat Real Madrid next week?"

He gave me a huge smile and said, "Oh yeah. We'll crush them!" (Too bad he was wrong.)

Now whenever I see him he waves, often from across the store. I almost always walk over, say hi, and talk briefly about soccer.

That's as far as our relationship is likely to go and that's okay. For a couple of minutes we transcend the customer/employee relationship and become two people brightening each other's day.

And that's enough, because every relationship, however minor and possibly fleeting, has value.

People who build great relationships treat every one of their relationships that way. (That's a lesson I need to take to heart more often.)

By building positive relationships with others, we will be happier and more fulfilled and feel more supported, supportive, and connected.

The most important single ingredient in the formula of success is knowing how to get along with people.—Theodore Roosevelt

One of the most profound experiences we can have in our lives is the connection we have with other human beings. Positive and supportive relationships will help us to feel healthier, happier, and more satisfied with our lives. So here are a few tips to help you to develop more positive and healthy relationships in all areas of your life:

1. Accept and celebrate differences. One of the biggest challenges we experience in relationships is that we are all different. We can perceive the world in many ways. Certainly astumbling block that we come across when we try to build relationships is a desire or an expectation that people will think like we do and, in this way, it is so much easier to create a rapport. We feel more comfortable when we feel that people "get" us and can see our

point of view. Life, however, would be very dull if we were all the same and, while we may find it initially easier, the novelty of sameness soon would wear off. So accepting and celebrating that we are all different is a great starting point.

2. Listen effectively. Listening is a crucial skill in boosting another person's self-esteem, the silent form of flattery that makes people feel supported and valued. Listening and understanding what others communicate to us is the most important part of successful interaction and vice versa.

Active or reflective listening is the single most useful and important listening skill. In active listening, we also are genuinely interested in understanding what the other person is thinking, feeling, wanting, or what the message means, and we are active in checking out our understanding before we respond with our own new message. We restate or paraphrase our understanding of their message and reflect it back to the sender for verification. This verification or feedback process is what distinguishes active listening and makes it effective.

3. Give people your time. Giving time to people is also a huge gift. In a world where time is of the essence and we are trying to fit in more than one lifetime, we don't always have the time to give to our loved ones, friends, and work colleagues. Technology has somewhat eroded our ability to build real rapport and we attempt to multi-task by texting and talking at the same time.

Being present in the time you give to people is also important, so that, when you are with someone, you are truly with someone and not dwelling in the past or worrying about the future. The connection we make with other people is the verytouchstone of our existence, and devoting time, energy, and effort to developing and building relationships is one of the most valuable life skills.

4. Develop your communication skills. Communication occurs when someone understands you, not just when you speak. One of the biggest dangers with communication is that we can work on the assumption that the other person has understood the message we are trying to get across.

Poor communication in the workplace can lead to a culture of back stabbing and blame, which, in turn, can affect our stress levels, especially when we don't understand something or feel we have been misled. It also can have a positive effect on morale when it works well and motivates individuals to want to come into work and do a great job.

5. Manage mobile technology. By now, pretty much everyone has a mobile phone and many people have two or more. While they are a lifesaver in an emergency, and an effective tool for communication, they also can be a complete distraction when people exhibit a lack of mobile phone etiquette.

6. Learn to give and take feedback. Feedback, in my opinion, is the food of progress, and while it may not always taste great, it can be very good for you. The ability to provide constructive feedback to others helps them to tap into their personal potential and can help to forge positive and mutually beneficial relationships. From your own personal perspective, any feedback you receive is free information and you can choose whether you want to take it on board or not. It can help you to tap into your blind spot and get a different perspective.

7. Learn to trust more. A long time ago, my brother and I had a philosophical debate about what was more important in a relationship—love, trust, or passion. I was a lot younger and more naive then and caught up in the heady rollercoaster of sensation seeking. I have grown to understand, however, that trust is hugely important in any relationship. Years later, I bought my brother a photograph of a little girl who was smiling and staring confidently at the camera with an elephant's foot just above her head. The caption was: "To trust is more important than love." I believe that sentiment is true because no love will last without equal amounts of respect and trust.

8. Develop empathy. There is a great expression that I learned a long time ago: "People will forget what you said, people will forget what you did, but people will never forget how you made them feel."

Empathy and understanding builds connection between people. It is a state of perceiving and relating to another person's feelings and needs without blaming, giving advice, or trying to fix the situation. Empathy also means "reading" another person's inner state and interpreting it in a way that will help the other person and offer support and develop mutual trust.

Every relationship we have can teach us something, and by building positive relationships with others, we will be happier and more fulfilled and feel more supported, supportive, and connected.

How to Build Good Work Relationships

• Ok, what can you do to create stronger working relationships?

• Build Your People's Skills • Good partnerships begin with good people's skills. Taking our How Strong Is The People Skills? Quiz to find out how the soft skills are. For example, how well you work together, connect, and cope with tension. This self-test will guide you to tools that can help you cope with any deficiencies you may have.

• Identify your partnership needs • Take a look at your own partnership conditions. Will you know what other people need? So do you know what you need?

• Considering these desires will be influential in creating a stronger partnership.

• Plan Time to Build Relationships • Devote a portion of the day to establishing relationships, even though it's just 20 minutes out, even broken up into five-minute chunks.

• For example, you might pop into someone's office at lunchtime, respond to people's Twitter or LinkedIn messages, or ask a friend for a fast cup of coffee.

• Such small encounters tend to create the basis for a healthy partnership, particularly if they are face-to-face.

• Emphasis on your EI• Even, spend some time building your emotional intelligence (EI). It is the power, among other aspects, to know your own feelings, and to hear precisely what they're telling you.

• High EI also lets you understand the feelings and desires of others.

• Appreciate Others • Express thanks if anyone supports you. Everybody, from the supervisor to the office cleaner, deserves to know like their job is appreciated. So, genuinely thank the people around you when they're doing a good job. It is going to open the door to better working relationships.

• Be positive • Focus on being optimistic. Positivity is appealing and infectious, and it can help to improve your relationship with your coworkers. One likes to be around someone who's pessimistic all the time.

• Maintain The Boundaries • Make sure that you create and handle limits properly—all of us want to have friends at work, but sometimes connections can have an effect on our careers, particularly when a friend or colleague starts monopolizing our time.

• If this occurs, it is crucial that you be assertive in your expectations, and that you know how much time you will expend on social media during your working day.

Stop Gossiping • Don't gossip—workplace politics and "whisper" are the biggest killers at work. If you have a disagreement with someone in your party, speak to them personally about the issue. Gossiping about the situation with other coworkers would only worsen the problem and cause distrust and resentment between you.

• Listen Regularly • Exercise constructive listening while communicating to your clients and colleagues. People are listening to others who actually listen to what they have to say. Focus on listening rather than you speak, and you can soon become recognized as someone you can trust.

Difficult Relationships

Sometimes, you're going to have to deal with someone you don't want, or someone you simply can't connect to. Nevertheless, for the sake of your career, it is important that you have a professional relationship with him.

When this happens, do your utmost to get to know the guy. She undoubtedly knows full well that the two of you are not on the same terms, so make the first step to strengthen the relationship by involving him in a serious discussion, or by asking him to lunch.

Seek not to be too defensive when you're talking. Ask him about his history, his interests and his past achievements. Instead of pouring effort into your differences, concentrate on seeking things you have in common.

Only note—not all marriages are going to be great; but you should make sure they're at least workable!

Relational Intelligence (RI) tells us that the way we want to respond to each other defines the nature of our human experience and shows what we trust most. Unless we take a panoramic perspective of society, we would find that human relationships are sadly frequently limited to goods, as if individuals were purchasing, selling, and exchanging relationships for personal gain.

Although many members aspire to be relationally knowledgeable, they fail to grasp what it entails and how it can be applied. "Relational" in RI means learning to treat others as the ultimate value and to express that value to them. The "Intelligent" aspect of RI involves learning strong leadership skills and then incorporating them in ways that maximize their impact.

Most organisations and their members face major problems in a complex and interconnected society. To operate effectively in the 21st century, leaders are faced with an legal challenge, a sustainability challenge, a strategic challenge and a stakeholder challenge. We also form their leadership positions and duties, which have a social aspect. The ability to engage with diverse people from various cultural contexts, both within and outside the organisation, with specific expectations and beliefs allows members to communicate and behave interpersonally and ethically competently.

We also recognize that leaders need cognitive intellibence to deal with the complexities of leadership both socially and ethically experienced. We describe relational intelligence as a mixture of emotional and ethical intelligence, which includes the capacity to be conscious of and consider one's own and others ' feelings, beliefs, desires and demands, to differentiate between them, to objectively focus on them, and to use this knowledge to direct one's actions and behaviour towards others.

Using case studies, we demonstrate how partnership intellibence (emotional and ethical) can direct leadership activity in relationships that help leaders cope with dynamic ethical and cultural dilemmas and make rational and reasonable decisions. It is believed that relational knowledge will help global leaders in addressing leadership challenges by leading them to communicate well across boundaries and to create healthy and trustworthy relationships with various stakeholders.

The application of micro-and macro-level relational intelligence will be a tool for both individuals and companies to cultivate partnerships, increase efficiency, strengthen collaboration / teamwork, increase transparency, boost employee engagement, boost worker satisfaction, and minimize costs within organizations.

www.ingramcontent.com/pod-product-compliance
Lightning Source LLC
Chambersburg PA
CBHW061039050726
47592CB00004B/1518